Welcome to the Royal Fusiliers Museum, one of the four museums of the Royal Regiment of Fusiliers.

I am especially proud of the Museum and its collection which brings to life and salutes the long and illustrious history of the Royal Fusiliers and more recently of the Royal Regiment of Fusiliers.

Evocative displays blend with historic memorabilia from long past conflicts and triumphs to make up a fascinating look at British and World History.

Housed in Her Majesty's Tower of London, the traditional home of the Regiment, and opened by Her Royal Highness Princess Marina, Duchess of Kent in November 1962, there could be no finer or more appropriate setting for a Museum of Military History.

I very much hope you enjoy your visit.

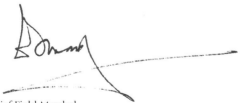

The Colonel-in-Chief Field Marshal
His Royal Highness The Duke of Kent KG

'keep up lads'

CONTENTS

Main picture (right):

A Fusil's firing mechanism

The Regiment took its name from the new style musket which had a covered flash pan to minimise the risk of sparks igniting the gunpowder used by the Artillery.

ORIGINS

'To our right trusty and well beloved counsellor, George Lord Dartmouth'. These words, dated 11th June 1685, introduce the commission given to Lord Dartmouth by King James II, to raise, as Colonel, 'Our Royal Regiment of Fusiliers'.

'keep up lads'

London 1685

The Museum's example of the original Fusil, from which The Regiment gained its name

ORIGINS OF THE REGIMENT

In June 1648 the Tower Guard was formed as part of The Trained Bands of The Tower of London and its Hamlets. The Regiment took the name of its Colonel and was also known as The Tower Regiment of Foot, and it formed part of Oliver Cromwell's New Model Army. On October 11th 1669 George Legge was appointed Captain of an Independent Company, and on December 7th 1670 he was appointed Lieutenant General of Ordnance, and Master General in March 1685, all within the Tower where the King's Ordnance was commissioned and manufactured. He also commanded a Regiment of Foot which bore his name from February 18th, 1678 to its disbandment in 1679. George Legge was appointed Constable of The Tower on May 2nd 1685 and as such he also had the additional role of Officer Commanding The Tower Hamlets Militia whose successors would become The 4th Volunteer Battalion Royal Fusiliers in 1903.

George Legge, Lord Dartmouth

On June 11th 1685 George Legge, now Lord Dartmouth, by Royal command raised the Ordnance Regiment soon to be styled at the King's pleasure *"Our Royal Regiment of Fuzileers"* from the Tower Guard to guard the Ordnance Train. The Independent Company of Miners, also within the Tower, was added to the establishment. Another Independent Company of Foot within the Tower was commanded by Robert St.Clair, and he was commissioned Major in *The Royal Regiment of Fuzileers*. In 1687 a Grenadier Company was authorised, and this also originated from The Independent Company of Grenadiers of the Tower Guard, commanded by Captain Cheek who was appointed on December 12th 1685. From 1685 to 1922 The Regiment had raised 70 Battalions of soldiers who wore the cap badge and distinctions of The Royal Fusiliers, The 7th Regt. of Foot, and later The City of London Regiment. From 1939 to 1955 a further 52 Battalions had the distinction of wearing the badge.

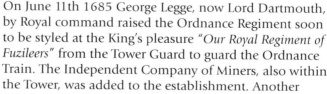

The uniform of an early Fusilier was scarlet coat lined with yellow, grey breeches and stockings and yellow cloth caps

THE ROYAL
REGIMENT OF
FUSILIERS
MUSEUM

INTO BATTLE FOR THE FIRST TIME

William III ascended to the English throne in 1688 after James II had exiled himself. That year the Regiment joined the Dutch Army to assist them in their war against France and took part in its first full scale action at Walcourt. The French were defeated and, as a reward for his leadership, Lord Marlborough was appointed Colonel of the Regiment in succession to Lord Dartmouth who had forfeited the post because of his loyalty to King James. Louis XIV was at war with most of Europe from 1688 to 1698 (the War of the League of Augsburg), and the action at Walcourt was the first of several battles which involved the Royal Fusiliers. With William's accession to the throne, the Fusiliers ceased to be an Ordnance Regiment and became a regular Infantry Regiment of the line.
In 1688, the Regiment consisted of 40 officers, 32 sergeants and 593 soldiers; the total wages bill was £14,000.

Fusiliers of 1688

Photo: Jeremy Whitaker

In 1690 the Fusiliers went to Ireland where they took part in the siege of Cork and captured Kinsale before spending three months in Garrison in Limerick

ACTION IN IRELAND AND FLANDERS

By 1690 the French were gaining the upper hand over the Dutch, and in January 1691 the Fusiliers returned to Flanders. In 1692 Marlborough having fallen under William's displeasure, was replaced as Colonel by Lord George Hamilton. Later he too was replaced by Colonel Edward Fitzpatrick. In 1693 the Regiment took part in the bloody battle of Landen and in 1695 gained its first Battle Honour by heroic action at the battle of Namur.

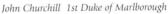

John Churchill 1st Duke of Marlborough

*Queen Anne
reigned 1702-1714*

By 1696 William was in trouble at home, and fearing an insurrection, he ordered many of his troops, including the Fusiliers, back to England. By the time they reached Gravesend, however, the danger had passed and the Fusiliers returned to Flanders without having set foot on English soil. In 1697 peace came at last and the Regiment returned to England. In August of the next year it proceeded to the Channel Islands of Jersey and Guernsey where it served until 1702. In the summer of that year, Queen Anne, now on the English throne, declared war against France and Spain. This became known as the War of the Spanish Succession (1702-1713).

Photo: Jeremy Whitaker

In 1695 The Regiment gained its first Battle Honour at the battle of Namur

RECRUITING AND TRAINING IN THE 18TH CENTURY

'Taking the King's Shilling' & 'Smart Money'

Although persuading men to join the Army was never easy, the Press Gang by which the Navy filled its ranks was never a feature of Army recruiting. In fact no matter how bad the situation, the Fusiliers continued to insist on some standards. In the 1750s Recruiting Sergeants were told that they could not enlist any man suffering *'rupture, scald head, crooked legs or inkneed'*. The regulations of the day were quite specific. *'The men enlisted are to be stout and well made, perfectly well-limbed, open-chested and long in the fork'*. Once enlisted, a man was to be taken before a Magistrate within four days to be sworn in. It was during that period, that the soldier might be able to bribe the Sergeant to let him go by paying *'Smart Money'*. All Regulations of the day warned officers to look out for the payment of money and to send all offenders for Court Martial.

A Fusilier in the late 18th century would be paid on enlistment the sum of £5. 14 shillings and given *'Necessaries'*, to the value of £3. 15 shillings. These *'Necessaries'* consisted of:

2 shirts	2 combs
2 pairs of shoes	2 pairs of stockings
1 pack	straps for greatcoat
2 leggings	stock and clasp

A further shilling was paid to the soldier on taking the oath, and this became known as the King's Shilling. The practice of drinking beer from a glass-bottomed tankard is said to originate with the King's Shilling. Legend has it that an unscrupulous Recruiting Sergeant would place a shilling in a likely lad's beer without him seeing it, and so cause the lad to *'Take the King's Shilling'*, and unwittingly enlist. The glass bottom would reveal such a trick. As the Sergeant was paid for each enlistment, such tricks were probable. Recruit training in the early days consisted almost entirely of marching, shooting and the adopting of tactical formations. This latter required a great deal of practising, being complicated and with great room for error. Weapon training in the 18th century was long and complicated.

Weapon training in the 18th century was long and complicated. Pocket books illustrating various movements of pike and musket were produced all over Europe

Courtesy of the Director, National Army Museum, London

PASSING IN REVIEW: QUICK TIME

A soldier of the 7th Regiment (or Royal 'Fuzileers') on parade duty during the 18th century is illustrated in this contemporary engraving, giving great detail as to the dress code and appropriate uniform

George Hamilton, Earl of Orkney KT - 1692

JOIN YOUR LEFT HAND TO YOUR FIRELOCK...'

Musket drill was equally complicated. The *'Complete Body of the Art Military'* published in the late 17th century gives twelve separate movements between *'Unshoulder your musket'*, to *'Give fire breast high'*. The writer of that manual devoted a great deal of space to explaining *'several reasons why the Pike is the more honourable weapon'*. The argument would appear to be similar to those used two hundred years later by officers who deplored the proposals to replace horses with tanks.

ARMY PAY AND PRIVILEGE IN THE 18TH CENTURY

A soldier enlisting in the 17th or 18th century was usually in the army for all his working days. He lived a life similar to his civilian counterpart, which meant in near squalor with drink playing a large part. He was often lodged in local inns, where food and accommodation were of a very low standard. Officers were appointed by patronage in the very early days, but this later changed to a system of purchase. In 1719 for instance, the going rate for various ranks was as follows:

Colonel and Captain	*£5,000*
Major and Captain	*£1,500*
Lieutenant	*£250*
Ensign	*£170*
Quartermaster	*£125*

This system was not abolished in the British Army until 1871.

There was no training for officers at that time, nor was any considered necessary; the ability to lead was thought to be as much inherited as the private income many of them enjoyed. It was well worth paying for a good rank in certain regiments, as the command of troops could be a lucrative business. Captains handled all the money due to their men, and in many cases contrived to retain part of it for their own use. Troops were seldom paid regularly and always in arrears. The exception to this state of affairs was the Duke of Marlborough, who, through the influence of his friend Godolphin, the Lord Treasurer, always had adequate resources for pay and supplies. James II made Lord Dartmouth Captain of a Fusilier Company as well as Colonel of the Regiment, so that he could have direct control of their pay.

ARMY LIFE AND PUNISHMENTS

Quite often regiments were seriously depleted by the large numbers being absent without leave, or away on recruiting drives, and the control was left in the hands of non-commissioned officers. Officers treated soldiers with a mixture of indifference and affectionate care when things went well, and severe punishment when they did not. A sentence of 500 lashes was not unusual and 200 lashes was a comparatively minor punishment. The following was written by Sergeant Cooper of the Fusiliers in the late 18th century; *'Flogging was by beat of drum and ten drum beats separated each stroke of the lash. Many were flogged into insensibility and one I saw, into insanity. It required strong nerves to look on, and indeed, many spectators fainted during prolonged punishments. One man I saw was later admitted to hospital with a wound 8" x 6" full of matter in which were a number of black-headed maggots striving to hide themselves'.*

*A Fusilier of
1742*

EUROPEAN CAMPAIGNS 1702-1773

'SERVICE ON BOARD THE FLEET'

At the outbreak of the War of Spanish Succession, the Regiment was ordered from the Channel Islands to England, to join a large force assembled at Cowes *'for service on board the fleet'*. The force embarked in July with orders to capture Cadiz, but it was decided not to concentrate on Cadiz itself, but to attack the rich but strategically unimportant and virtually undefended village of Port Saint Mary. Bad weather hampered the landing and about 20 Fusiliers were drowned. Having taken the town, the mixed force of soldiers and sailors set about systematically plundering the twin villages of Port Saint Mary and Rota, in one of the less illustrious episodes in the Regiment's history. Over the following month, discipline almost completely collapsed and officers as well as men, devoted themselves to the gathering of booty. An assault on the well-defended Cadiz was now deemed impracticable and the expedition re-embarked for England without military achievement. On the voyage home it was learnt that the Spanish galleons, or treasure ships, were anchored at Vigo under the protection of a French convoy, and course was immediately set for Vigo. Though the French Admiral made a vigorous defence, and ordered his ships to be set on fire when his position became hopeless, ten men-of-war and eleven galleons packed with treasure, were captured by the Allied force, who thus redeemed their expedition, earning the sincere gratitude of their sovereign Queen Anne.

Gibraltar was captured by the British under Sir George Rooke, 2nd August 1704. Together with Minorca, it helped the Royal Navy to dominate the Western Mediterranean

'THE SIEGE OF LERIDA'

Shortly after the battle of Almanza, the Regiment joined the Allied garrison at Lérida to which the enemy soon laid siege. The slender garrison held out for a month against fierce assaults but eventually was dislodged and forced to retire to a castle behind the town. Here the Allied Force held out for a further month, defending themselves vigorously, but finally water and provisions were entirely exhausted. Reduced to barely five hundred men, the garrison capitulated

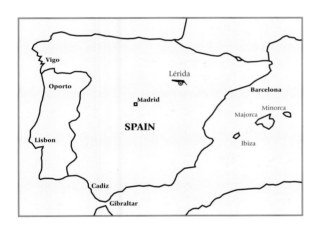

As a Regiment, the Royal Fusiliers had been virtually destroyed, but the brave and bloody resistance they and their fellow soldiers had maintained, won for them the most advantageous terms and the high respect of their captors. The remnant of the garrison marched out of Lérida on 12th November 1707 with colours flying and heads held high

WAR OF THE SPANISH SUCCESSION 1702-1713

Louis XIV of France claimed the whole Spanish Empire for his grandson. This disturbed the balance of power in Europe. He also supported the Stuarts as rightful Kings of Scotland, in place of William III. He was opposed by the Grand Alliance of England, Holland, the Emperor of the Holy Roman Empire, and the King of Prussia. England and Holland were also anxious to reduce France's maritime trading power. Compromise was reached in 1713 - *The Treaty of Utrecht* - which resolved the crisis and Great Britain emerged holding the balance of power in Europe, while building up an empire in India and North America.

After three years of home service, the Royal Fusiliers were ordered to Gibraltar in 1706 and were at once transferred to Men-of-War and set sail for Barcelona which was besieged by the French. Though the French had suffered heavy losses over the previous weeks, they now had the upper hand and a final assault on the garrison was hourly expected. The arrival of the Allied fleet completely altered the situation and the French Admiral was left with little alternative but to abandon the siege. This he duly did on May 11th while the sun was under a total eclipse. His troops retired in hurry and confusion and left behind them vast quantities of guns, mortars, ammunition and stores, in addition to their sick and wounded whom they recommended to the humanity of the British Soldier.

In 1773 the Fusiliers were sent to Quebec and later to St. Johns in Lower Canada with a small outpost at Fort Chamblé. At the beginning of the War of Independence in 1777, and in the hope of persuading their Canadian neighbours to turn against the British, the Americans attempted to capture Montreal and Quebec. They infiltrated along the valleys leading to the St. Lawrence River, capturing isolated British forts as they did so. One of these forts was St. Johns. A party of their few Canadian allies, by a stroke of luck, captured Fort Chamblé and with it the Colours of the Fusiliers. Those very Colours are displayed to this day in the Military Academy at West Point. The defeat at Fort Chamblé led to a similar result at St. Johns. The Americans went on to capture Montreal where the bulk of the Regiment was based. However, a subsequent siege of Quebec failed and the captive Fusiliers were exchanged in time to help recapture Montreal and drive the Americans out of Canada.

December 1775 - having successfully led American forces to the gates of Quebec, Colonel Montgomery was killed as he attempted to capture the city. His troops were beaten and retreated from Canada

Picture courtesy of the Director, National Army Museum, London

John Andre & Benedict Arnold

Benedict Arnold was, and still is, considered to be the archetypal American traitor. He surrendered West Point to the British, and even today, the phrase *"a real Benedict Arnold"* is still in common usage. John Andre, an officer of the 7th, was the go-between who crossed the lines several times at great danger to himself to conduct negotiations with Arnold. To avoid being classed as a spy in the event of capture Andre always crossed in uniform as he did on the last occasion. Unfortunately however prior to his return, on a filthy night, he was persuaded to don a civilian greatcoat over his uniform. He was captured on his way back, tried as a spy, and hanged! Arnold went on to enjoy the life of a gentleman in England supported by a generous pension from the British.

The British Government had many disagreements with the American Colonists, most of whom were descendants of immigrants who had arrived over a hundred years before and regarded Britain as remote and foreign.

'keep up lads'

1777- 1783

A Fusilier of 1792

THE AMERICAN WAR OF INDEPENDENCE
1777-1783 - VICTORY & DEFEAT

When taxes were imposed by the British Government to help pay for defending them against the French and Indians, great resentment was aroused. An unfortunate skirmish at Lexington between British troops and Massachusetts Volunteers finally sparked off the war. It ended in triumph for the Colonists when British forces surrendered in Yorktown, 1781.

In 1777 the Fusiliers were in Philadelphia during an inglorious time for British Arms. It is recorded that 'gaming was permitted to a ruinous extent, the misconduct of officers offended the Philadelphians and made rebels of people originally loyal'. Worse perhaps was the military inactivity which allowed 4,000 American troops to remain in an almost helpless condition within 26 miles without the slightest molestation. On 18th June 1777 the British Army, alarmed by French support for the Americans, retreated to New York. Two years later in December 1779 the Fusiliers set sail for South Carolina to attack Charleston. The attack succeeded and in May 1780 the town surrendered with the loss or capture of ten American Regiments, three battalions of artillery and the local militia. The Fusiliers, more experienced by now, lost one killed and one wounded.

The battle of Cowpens in 1781 was significant in that for the first time British Regulars were beaten in a set battle by American Irregulars. 'As the British drew near, the Americans faced about and gave close and murderous fire. Stunned, the British recoiled in confusion and the Americans charged with the bayonet, so gaining the day.' For the Fusiliers, this was their last battle of that particular war. The Regiment was all but destroyed.

The American victory at Cowpens was the beginning of the end. Their readiness to adopt new tactics at the expense of the more rigid parade-ground type drills of the British paid off. The Militia, all expert shots and armed with the much superior rifle, gained confidence. Not for the first time was it proved, as it was to be proved in a later American War, that the tactics and weapons which gain the victory in one war, will not necessarily prove victorious in the next.

In 1783 the Fusiliers returned to Great Britain to spend 7 years in England and Scotland. On St. George's day 1789, HRH Edward Duke of Kent (1767 - 1820), was appointed to command The Regiment and so began the Royal connection which continues to this day

Right: HRH Edward Duke of Kent was the father of HM Queen Victoria

By courtesy of the National Portrait Gallery, London

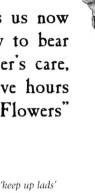

"For Royal Edward leaves us now
Twas he who taught us how to bear
The Soldier's toil, the leader's care,
Yet cheered fatigue with festive hours
And strewed war's rugged path with Flowers"

'keep up lads'

ROYAL COMMAND

'A ROYAL COLONEL IN COMMAND'

The Regiment went to Gibraltar and the new Colonel soon made his presence felt. It was said that *'Great slackness existed but the young Duke exacted a proper duty from each of his subordinates. His notion of discipline rendered him unpopular with his Fusiliers, and enemies on the Rock were striving to create discord in his Regiment. Ere long however, the tightening hand was felt to be that of a benefactor and his merits were appreciated by the whole garrison'.*

Edward took his Regiment to Canada in August 1791 and the Regiment remained there until 1802 when it was posted to the West Indies. In 1804 a Second Battalion was raised in the UK whilst the First Battalion remained in Bermuda and the Bahamas. By 1807 both Battalions were in England but Napoleon's attempt to seize the Danish Fleet and use it against England led to the Battle of Copenhagen in which the Fusiliers took part. Although a victory, it was hardly a glorious one and all Fusiliers were together in England by the end of the year.

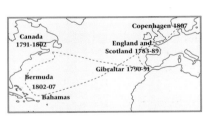

Movements of the Fusiliers 1783-1807

The Museum's display case features The Duke of Kent's swords, epaulettes, and Regimental egg cups, a silver beer tankard and a monogrammed dinner service

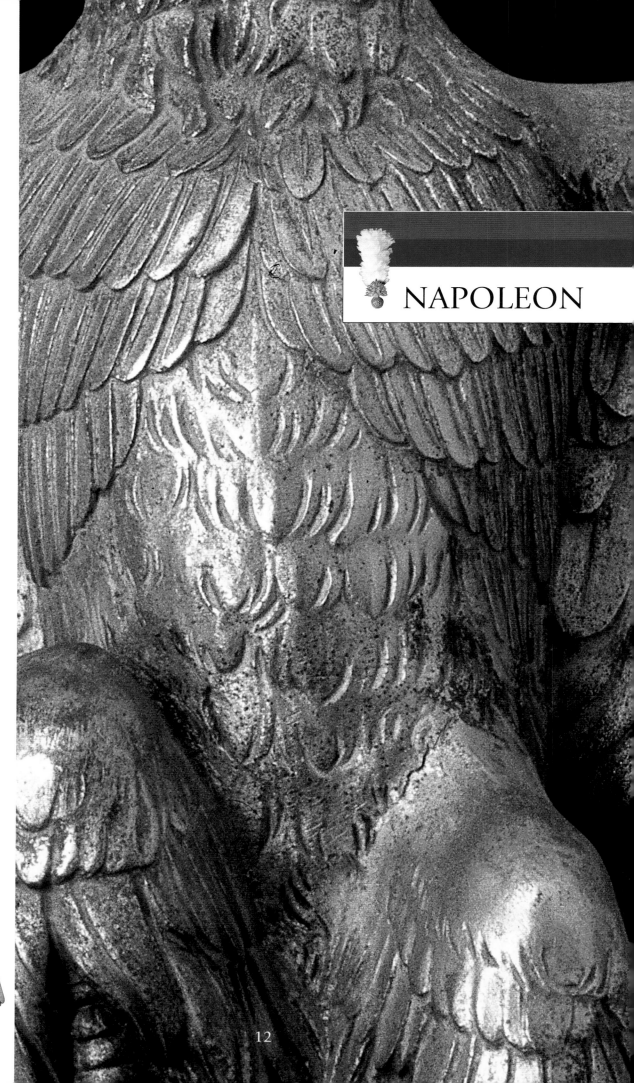

THE ROYAL REGIMENT OF FUSILIERS MUSEUM

THE CAPTURE OF MARTINIQUE

AND THE FRENCH EAGLE

The Fusiliers landed in Martinique, West Indies, on 30th January 1809 and were immediately engaged by the French, who after a gallant fight retired to Fort Bourbon. After a heavy few days bombardment of the Fort the French surrender on 23rd February. Three Eagles, the equivalent of British Colours, were captured and the Fusiliers, as a reward for their brave efforts, were allowed to keep the Eagle of the 82nd Regiment of the French Line which is displayed in the Museum

In 1802, after 11 years service in Canada, or British North America as it was then called, the Regiment was ordered to the West Indies, one half to Bermuda and the other to the Bahamas. The men suffered badly from sickness, but otherwise their stay was uneventful.

'keep up lads'

1796 - 1815

Below, a detail from:
'The BOMBARDMENT of COPENHAGEN and SURRENDER of the DANISH FLEET; to the BRITISH FORCES, September, 1807'

THE NAPOLEONIC WARS 1796-1815

'THE THREAT OF NAPOLEON'

Throughout this time, it was obvious that Napoleon Bonaparte was preparing to invade England, and consequently, war against France was declared in May 1803. Parliament readily consented to an augmentation of the army, and in July of the following year the 2nd Battalion Royal Fusiliers was reformed. Both Battalions were united briefly in England in 1806, but in November of that year the 1st Battalion was sent to Dublin.

Shortly afterwards it took part in the bombardment by sea of Copenhagen and the consequent capture of the Danish fleet, which Napoleon had intended to employ against England. The 2nd Battalion remained in England and was used mainly as a source of reinforcements for the 1st Battalion which had returned briefly to Canada after the Copenhagen expedition.

Courtesy of the Director, National Army Museum, London

'THE IMPORTANCE OF THE WEST INDIES'

The islands of the West Indies had been colonised in the 17th and 18th centuries mainly by England and France. During the Napoleonic Wars the islands were a major source of French wealth due to their sugar and coffee plantations. To cut this important economic life-line, the British Prime Minister, Pitt, ordered attacks to be made against the French possessions. These actions met with only limited success and more troops died of yellow fever (known as the black vomit), than fell victim to shot and sword

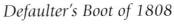

Defaulter's Boot of 1808

A gruesome reminder of army punishments meted out to defaulters in the past:
'Found of great use in the case of W. Reginauld after imposing on the Regiment for 3 years and 6 months was cured in 12 days by locking his leg in this box preventing him applying some corrosive substance which kept the sore open and was found on him being proved he was sentenced to 5 hundred lashes by a Regimental Court Martial Jersey 12th May 1808' Copied from the Original by order of J Clitherow Esq. - Colonel

PENINSULA

TALAVERA

BUSACO

BADAJOZ

ALBUHERA

SALAMANCA

VITTORIA

PYRENEES

ORTHES

TOULOUSE

PENINSULA

*The Military General
Service Medal
1793 - 1814*

14

When Portugal alone of the European Continental Nations refused to accept Napoleon's trade restrictions, a French army advanced through Spain and occupied Portugal.

'keep up lads'

1809- 1814

Napoleon's announcement that Spain was to be annexed and its King replaced, infuriated the Spaniards. England, glad to find anyone willing to oppose the French, even the old enemy Spain, promised money and assistance.

THUS BEGAN THE PENINSULAR WAR.

The Museum's diorama depicting the dramatic battle of Albuhera

Engaged in the blockade of Badajoz on 16th May 1811, the Fusiliers were suddenly told to march towards Albuhera.

Straight from 36 hours on picket duty and following a 20 mile night march, the Fusiliers arrived to find the battle going badly. The retreat had been ordered and the French held the heights and were poised to roll up the whole British Line. Two battalions of the Fusiliers together with a battalion of the 23rd Foot (now the Royal Welch Fusiliers), advanced up the hill. The historian Napier, takes up the story.

'A fearful discharge of grape whistled through the ranks, the Commanding Officers of all three battalions fell wounded and the Fusiliers, struck by that iron tempest reeled and staggered like sinking ships. Suddenly and sternly recovering, they closed upon their terrible enemies and then was seen, with what strength and majesty the British soldier fights. Nothing could stop that astonishing infantry. The rain flowed in streams coloured by blood and fifteen hundred unwounded Fusiliers, the remnant of four thousand, stood triumphant upon that fateful hill!'

Of all the ten battle honours awarded to the Regiment in the Peninsular Campaign, the name Albuhera is one of the proudest borne on the Colours. Albuhera Day is celebrated by the Regiment on 16th May each year and from that day to this, Officers and sergeants of the Fusiliers and the Royal Welch Fusiliers, have been members of each others messes.

ALBUHERA

16th May. 1811

VICTORY IN SPAIN

At the beginning of January 1812, the Fusiliers were once again engaged in the unrewarding business of siege warfare. They helped take Ciudad Rodrigo by storm and, in April, were part of the force which laid siege to the important city of Badajoz.

Courtesy of the Director, National Army Museum, London

'A view of the SIEGE and STORMING of CIUDAD RODRIGO in SPAIN on JANUARY 19th 1812

This place and its fortifications were taken by storm after dark by the gallant British and Allied forces commanded by General Lord Wellington who in half an hour were complete masters of the whole, and made prisoners the Governor General Banier and about 78 officers and 1700 men, besides 153 pieces of Ordnance and a great quantity of stores and Ammunition taken by the Victors'.

The battle of Badajoz

On the evening of April 6th, two parties of Fusiliers entered the breaches below Badajoz, but after a terrific explosion, they were subjected to a hail of fire. Many of those who survived the French fire did so only to die in the dark, choked and smothered in mud, in a narrow ditch which the enemy had dug specially. Out of chaos finally came victory, but at a high cost. By the middle of 1812 the initiative in the war began to pass to the British, and with a tremendous victory at the Battle of Salamanca, in which the performance of the Fusiliers was conspicuous, the

Courtesy of the Director, National Army Museum, London

scent of the ultimate British victory hung in the air. At Salamanca the British 4th Division, of which the Fusiliers formed a part, delivered a crushing blow to the army of the French General Marmont. 'We fell upon Marmont', said Wellington, 'and I never saw an army receive such a beating'. In June Napoleon's army was routed at Vittoria. The 4th Division pursued the French up into the cold heights of the Pyrenees, engaging them again on July 28th at Pampeluna. This was another, albeit costly, victory for the Fusiliers, and again Wellington praised his men, 'who have so frequently been distinguished in this army', for surpassing even their former good conduct.

Above and below: An officer's gilt Colour belt plate, and The Regiment's Peninsular campaign Honours

THE MYERS MINIATURE

The Myers miniature commemorates Royal Fusilier Officers killed in the Peninsula War 1809 - 1814. Lieutenant-Colonel Sir William Myers died aged 27, commanding the Fusilier Brigade at Albuhera, 16 May 1811

In 1814, the armies entered France itself. The Fusiliers fought and won two more battles, at Orthes in February and at Toulouse in April, and on April 12th Napoleon abdicated. The Regiment had won no less than ten battle honours for its Colours in just over five years.

Gift to Rev. Wallace from HRH Prince Edward, Colonel of the Regiment

At the conclusion of the Peninsular Campaign, the Regiment was despatched to America where it fought at the Battle of New Orleans.

*Detail of a coatee
circa 1825*

*Colonel Frederick
Farquharson
Royal Fusiliers, 1825*

PEACE

PACE
BONUS
ET
UTILIS

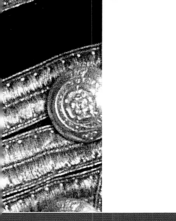

The Fusiliers left America for England and on the voyage heard the news that Napoleon had escaped from Elba and had made his way back to France. After two weeks at home, the Regiment embarked at Ramsgate to join Wellington's army in Belgium, landing at Ostend on the very day that Napoleon was defeated at Waterloo.

'keep up lads'

Field Marshal Sir Edward Blakeney, the 14th Colonel of The Royal Fusiliers served with great distinction in the Peninsular War, and became the Senior Field Marshal of the British Army. He died in 1868

1815- 1854

The Fusiliers spent time as part of the 'Army of Occupation' in Paris, Bapaume, Boulon and Valenciennes and returned to England in November 1818.

'CHEERFUL, COLOURFUL OCCASIONS'

In the years between Waterloo and the Crimea, the activities of the Regiment were leisurely and gentle typical of the general military decay of the period. They attended King George IV in his exuberant Pavilion in Brighton in 1822, spent time in Corfu, and in a glorious parade under the hot Maltese sun, had new colours presented to the Regiment by Lady Augusta Fitzclarence in 1829. Time was also spent in Ireland on general peace keeping duties. In 1836 the Fusiliers received a special mark of royal favour at Windsor, when King William IV presented them with a gift of silver for the officers' mess table. The King also absolved officers of the Royal Fusiliers from drinking the Loyal Toast. A tradition they observe to this day.

Silver wine cooler presented to the Royal Fusiliers in 1836 by HM King William IV at Windsor Castle - this beautiful piece of silver is still in use today at functions in the Officers' Mess at Regimental Headquarters, HM Tower of London

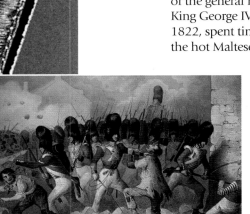

'REBUILDING IN GIBRALTAR'

Even when the Regiment went abroad, military affairs seemed far away, and it is a sign of the times that the Fusiliers, during their stay in Gibraltar in 1842, were employed to build a road on Windmill Hill. "Pace bonus et utilis" (In peace, law-abiding and useful), is how the Regiment is described on a tablet commemorating this work.

Above left: A contemporary aquatint of The Royal Fusiliers quelling civil unrest in their own country - United Kingdom

Left: The imposing Rock of Gibraltar

21

THE ROYAL REGIMENT OF FUSILIERS MUSEUM

CRIMEA

An extract from a letter home - 'My dear parents...grape and canister came amongst us like hail. Up the hill we went step by step amidst fearful carnage...the smoke of the battle was so great we could not see and our poor fellows were falling all around...the fighting was desperate but we reached the top and took the Russian battery...forced half way down the hill again but Victory was soon ours. Dear parents what a sight the whole field is. I hope you can read this scrawl because my only table is a dead Russian...I thank God with a sincere heart for protecting me. From your rough but affectionate son'.
T. Gowing, Royal Fusiliers

Crimea Medal
Sebastopol, Inkerman
Alma 1854-56

From the Will of Peter the Great

'In the name of the Holy and Indivisible Trinity, we, Peter and Emperor of all Russia to all our successors...providence has evidently designed Russia to be the Conqueror and ruler of all Europe.'

'keep up lads'

1854- 1856

THE CRIMEAN WAR

With the decay of the Turkish Empire, Russia saw her chance to improve her access to the Mediterranean. Using as a pretence, a quarrel over the rights of Christians in the Holy Places of Jerusalem, Russia invaded Turkey. Britain and France went to Turkey's aid, declared war and landed troops at Varna on the Black Sea.

In October the Regiment embarked upon Steamers and on the 14th they landed in Kalamita Bay. The invasion of the Crimea had begun but, as so often with the British Army, at the beginning of battle the men were ill-equipped. Sergeant Major Gowing tells us. 'The French and the Turks had their tents but there were none for us. Thousands of British sons who had come to fight for Queen and Country were thrown ashore without shelter of any kind'.

RUSSIA

CRIMEA

Sebastopol   Alma

BLACK SEA   Balaclava

A battered bugle from the period

A contemporary lithograph illustrating Officers' dress of the Crimean period

Officer's mess jacket
and forage cap

THE ROYAL
REGIMENT OF
FUSILIERS
MUSEUM

AN EYE WITNESS ACCOUNT OF THE BATTLE OF THE ALMA

'There were 14 guns in front of us and others on our flanks. In all, some 42 guns were raining death and destruction on us. Into the battery we jumped, spiked the guns and bayoneted or shot the gunners but we were not strong enough; an overwhelming force hurled us out of the battery and down the hill again. We had lost more than half our men, dead or wounded, and our Colour was gone, but thank God the enemy did not have it. It was found upon the field cut and torn and with a heap of dead and wounded all around it. "A Victory, but at a price", our poor old Colonel exclaimed at the top of the hill, "a Colour gone and where's my poor old Fusiliers? My God!", and he cried like a child'.

Cannonballs from Alma

**The death of Colonel
Lacy Yea**

With the Battle of Inkerman began the unprecedented miseries endured by the British Army as it kept watch over the Russian garrison of Sebastopol. The Battle had proved nothing other than that once again the British Soldier had redeemed by heroic bravery the faults of his superiors in choosing to take up a position militarily untenable. But worse was to come. In June the following year, the Fusiliers were involved in an abortive attempt to capture a strongly defended earthworks at Sebastopol called the Redan. They suffered 87 casualties including their Colonel, Lacy Yea, who was killed by grape-shot as he led his men against the Russian guns

The ruins of Sebastopol

'THE TERRIBLE MORNING OF 5TH NOVEMBER'

In early November 1854, the Fusiliers were besieging Sebastopol, when the Russians attempted to break out prompting the Battle of Inkerman on 'the terrible morning of 5th November'. The Fusiliers under Colonel Lacy Yea were as usual foremost in the fray. The battle was a series of hand-to-hand combats where science and the tactics of war were ignored. The Fusiliers gained ground by an incessant slaughter of their foes and in the damp hillsides of Inkerman they helped gain the victory but at a fearful cost.

The Museum's diorama evoking the Battle of the Alma

LIEUTENANT HOPE
WINS THE VC

Willaim Hope, Lieutenant. 7th Regt.

After the troops had retreated on the morning of the 18th June 1855, Lieutenant W. Hope being informed by Sgt Major William Bacon, who was himself wounded, that Lieutenant and Adjutant Hobson was outside the trenches badly wounded, went out to look for him, and found him lying in an old agricultural ditch running towards the left flank of the Redan. He then returned and got four men to bring him in. Finding however that Lieutenant Hobson could not be moved without a stretcher, he then ran back across the open ground to Egerton's Pit, where he procured one, and carried it back to where Hobson was lying. All this was done under a heavy fire from the Russian batteries. Lieutenant Hope received his Victoria Cross personally from HM Queen Victoria in Hyde Park 26th June 1857.

In 1893 a submission was made to The War Office on behalf of Lieutenant Hope claiming a bar to the Victoria Cross in respect of his bravery at the French magazine explosion of November 1855. The submission was rejected under Clause V of the Royal Warrant relating to granting of second awards.

The Victora Cross - Britain's highest military honour. Each medal is created from a Russian gun captured during the Crimean War

POLICING

THE INDIAN GENERAL SERVICE MEDAL 1854 -1895 "UMBEYLA"

This medal with the clasp "UMBEYLA" was awarded for the operations on The North West Frontier of India between October 20th and December 23rd 1863. These operations were conducted against the Hindustani tribes in Sittana and their village of Malka.The Euzofzai Field Force commanded by Brigadier General Sir Neville Chamberlain entered the Umbeyla Pass and Chamia Valley, where it met opposition beyond its powers to subdue. Reinforcements were dribbled out to it until November, during which month the Commander was seriously wounded when leading a counter attack against the famous Crag Picquet. Eventually the Commander-in-Chief Sir Hugo Rose decided to send further reinforcements and appointed Major General Garvock to succeed Chamberlain. The troops were organised into two brigades which drove the Hindustanis out of the valley, and then a small party under Colonel Reynell-Taylor with an escort of Guides went forward and burned Malka. In this expedition the British suffered 900 casualties,and incidentally gained a good deal of knowledge in carrying out this sort of warfare against stubborn hill fighters. When things were not going so well the C.-in-C. sent Major Frederick Roberts, R.A. later Field Marshal Lord Roberts of Kandahar into the district to make an appreciation of the situation, which he did with that accuracy and charm that signalised his career to come

The Indian Mutiny broke out at Meerut on May 10th, 1857, and as soon as the news reached England, reinforcements including the 1st Battalion The Royal Fusiliers, were hurried out. This was the first appearance of the Regiment in India, but by the time it had arrived the worst of the rebellion was over.

'keep up lads'

THE EMPIRE

Colours presented to the 1st Battalion Royal Fusiliers, July 1876

THE INDIAN MUTINY & FRONTIER CAMPAIGNS (1857-1880)

1st Battalion Royal Fusiliers, Peshawar, India 1864

The final stage of the war was fought in central India, and after fighting of intense savagery, the rebellion was finally crushed at the end of 1859. The Fusiliers saw little of this action however, having been sent to occupy the Punjab, where it was imperative that British troops should be maintained to ensure that the population remained passive.

Although the Fusiliers suffered badly from cholera at times, their stay in India was characterised by long stretches of peaceful inactivity punctuated by short, intense periods of campaigning. One officer described a typical Indian day:

'Early parade - breakfast - Orderly Room and a visit to the company, where we hang about until the C.O. has gone home - lunch - sleep until 4pm, then polo or tennis - and sunset drinks at the Club till we return to the mess for dinner.'

In an atmosphere of peaceful inactivity the occasional campaign came as a pleasant relief, and there were frequent, local clashes along the Northwest Frontier, such as that at Umbeyla in 1863, in which the Fusiliers successfully took part.

SERIOUS SQUABBLES

CANADA 1866 - 67

Between 31st May and 3rd June 1866 Fenian Raiders, (formerly The Irish National Militia), under the command of the self-styled Colonel John O'Neill, crossed the Niagara River and defeated the Canadian Militia at Ridgeway before withdrawing back into New York State. As a result more than 20,000 Militia men were called out. The British Garrison in Canada and the Maritime Provinces were put under arms, and in a state of alert, and reinforcements were at once dispatched. The Battalion left Quebec on 3rd June to take up duties in the field as a consequence of the Fenian raids into Canada. The Fenians having been subdued, the battalion returned to Quebec on 19th June.

Canada 1866, Field Force Camp at St.Amand

The Canada General Service Medal was approved by HM Queen Victoria in 1899 and issued by the Canadian Government some thirty years after the campaign. It was issued to all surviving claimants, although it was felt by some who had seen the privations of The Crimean War to be worthless. The medal roll may reflect this apathy, as it is known to be incomplete. The time lapse did nothing to improve the status of the medal.

Brantford, Canada, 1866 -
Royal Fusiliers on parade in the Town Square with Kirby House barracks and Town Hall

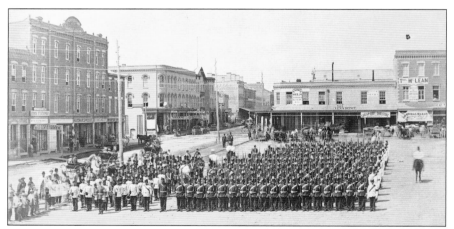

The local weekly newspaper welcomed The Royal Fusiliers, but went to great lengths to point out that:

"The girls of these parts are all engaged, and the redcoats are expected to take due notice, and behave accordingly !"

The Battalion was given a rousing send off with no reports of bad behaviour and no additions being claimed on the ration strength of the battalion.
It embarked for England on the 24th July on board HMT Belgian, having been replaced by five companies of the 17th Regiment. The Battalion arrived at Spithead on 8th August and on the 9th disembarked for quarters in Fort Grange, Rownen, Gomer, and Gosport.

AFGHANISTAN 1880

Sometimes local squabbles turned serious. Britain had long suspected that Russia had designs on Afghanistan, and, via Afghanistan, on India itself, and consequently tried to impose a treaty upon the Ameer of Afghanistan in 1878. This was rejected and then, after a British force had entered the country, accepted; but shortly afterwards the British Envoy in Kabul, with his staff and escort, were murdered. The British set out to avenge these deaths and in August 1880 the Royal Fusiliers found themselves part of a garrison attempting to hold Kandahar against a large Afghan force. The 2nd Battalion formed the backbone of the defence at Kandahar and greatly distinguished itself. Although the position was dangerous and the fighting fierce, the siege became known for many examples of individual heroism. Eventually the garrison was relieved by General Roberts, after his famous march from Kabul, and the Afghans were finally defeated at the Battle of Kandahar. Pte Thomas Ashford won his Victoria Cross in this action.

The Afghan War Medal with Kandahar bar

EGYPT 1882-86

On November 17th 1881 the 1st Battalion. Royal Fusiliers moved by rail from Pembroke Dock and Newport to take up quarters at HM Tower of London. On November 24th the battalion was inspected by Major General G.W.Higginson, CB, Commanding Home District. On July 29th 1882 a portion of the 1st Class Army Reserve was re-called in consequence of an expedition being sent to Egypt to suppress the rebellion by Arabi Pasha against the Khedive, and seventy reservists re-joined the 1st Battalion at The Tower of London. Lieut.Colonel F. Keyser, who had been promoted to the 1st Battalion. formed and commanded a Corps of Army Signallers, and Major G. Barton a Corps of Military Foot Police, each serving with their respective commands throughout the coming campaign.

A Guard of Royal Fusiliers on inspection in front of General Gordon's palace at Khartoum

The Khartoum trumpet

Early in December 1885 orders were received to prepare to move to Egypt to join the Army of Occupation, and on 9th December Lady Adye, wife of The Governor General of Gibraltar, presented new Colours to the battalion. The old Colours were returned to the Regimental Depot at Hounslow. The battalion broke camp at Abbasseyeh at the end of October and returned to Cairo, then proceeded up the Nile to Assuan.The country being in a settled state, the withdrawal of British troops from Upper Egypt commenced early in 1887, and on 25th March the battalion proceeded down the Nile en-route for Cairo.On the first night after leaving Assuan Colour Sgt. Ernest Silliphant fell overboard whilst sleep-walking and was drowned. His body being recovered and buried at Assuan. On December 7th the Mounted Infantry section rejoined the battalion, and received complimentary reports from Lieut. Colonel Barrow DSO, commanding the Mounted Infantry troops in Egypt. Early in January 1888 the battalion left Cairo for Suez where it embarked on board HMS Euphrates for Bombay.

A Glengarry

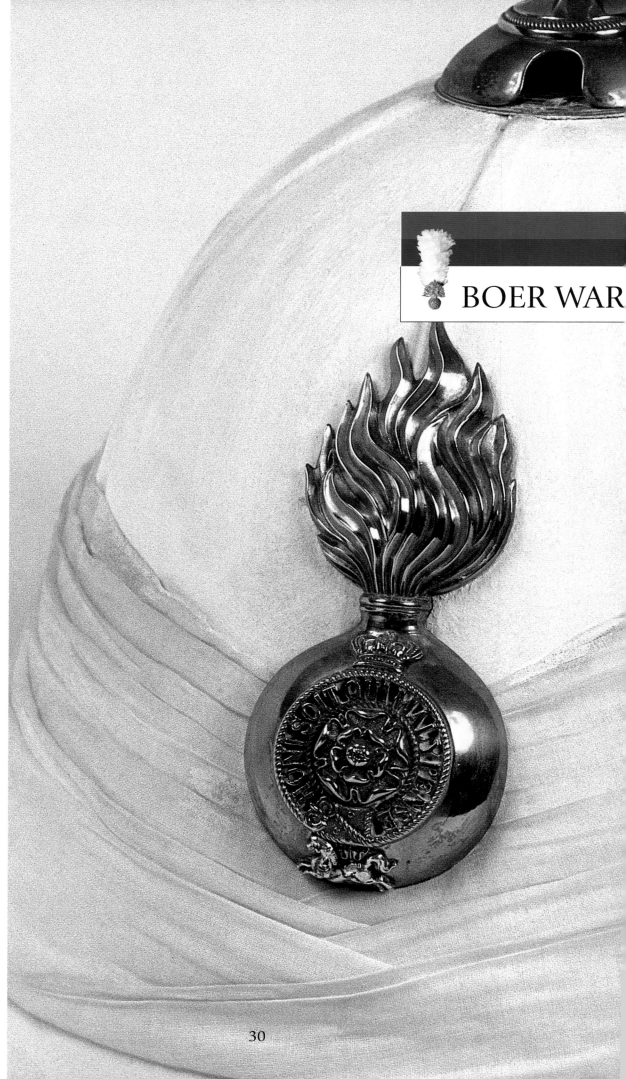

Lord Roberts in Command: Britain was forced to mobilise an enormous army and contingents were also sent from the self-governing Dominions, but the war rapidly turned in its favour. When the British commander Lord Roberts entered Pretoria, the capital of the Transvaal, on June 5th 1900, the resistance of the Boers appeared to be broken and the aged President Kruger fled to Europe. On October 25th the Transvaal and the Orange River were officially annexed to the British Empire. The Boers however continued to fight on and there was a long period of hard guerrilla warfare until they finally signed conditions of surrender in May of 1902. The 2nd Battalion of The Regiment won the following honours for its Colours: 'Relief of Ladysmith' and 'South Africa, 1899-1902'.

Queen's South Africa Medal 1899-1902

Over several years the Dutch settlers in southern Africa, or Boers, who had never accepted British laws kindly, had gradually moved north and after numerous wars with native tribes had founded two colonies, the Transvaal and Orange River.

'keep up lads'

1899-1902

2nd Battalion Royal Fusiliers disembarking in South Africa from the ship Pavonia, joining troop trains for the Front - "This fine body of men left England on October 22nd 1899, and have seen a lot of fighting"

SOUTH AFRICA

In 1881 the Boers' demands for total independence led to fighting with British troops and eventually the British Government recognised the two Republics, with reservations. The discovery of gold and diamonds and the formation of powerful mining corporations in the adjacent British colonies, which also deigned to exploit the territories of the Republics, led to continual friction, culminating in the notorious Jameson Raid of 1896 and the German Emperor's famous telegram of congratulation to President Kruger on the defeat of the raiders.

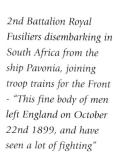

Officers' Bearskin badges; Volunteers' wore silver - Regular Officers' wore gilt

THE ROYAL FUSILIERS IN SOUTH AFRICA

The friction between Britain and the Boers turned to outright war in 1899 and a British Expeditionary Force, including the 2nd Battalion of the Royal Fusiliers, was dispatched to the Cape. The Boers, with great confidence in their own considerable abilities, struck first. They immediately proved themselves a force to be reckoned with, tying down 10,000 British soldiers in Ladysmith, and more in Kimberley and Mafeking, the relief of which became the primary British objective of the first part of the war. Sadly Queen Victoria died in 1901 and the King's South Africa Medal replaced the Queen's South Africa Medal.

King's South Africa Medal 1901-1902

31

In 1903 the British detected signs of Russian interference in Tibet. The country had long been isolated and xenophobic, but in 1903 its leader, the Dalai Lama, received into the 'forbidden city' of Lhasa, which supposedly no foreigner was permitted to enter, a so-called Russian trade mission.

'keep up lads'

TIBET　　　　　1904

THE YOUNGHUSBAND EXPEDITION OF 1904

Determined to resist Russian influence on the borders of India, the British dispatched a mission from Darjeeling, commanded by Colonel Young-husband and protected by a strong escort of Indian troops. The Tibetans fought poorly but obstinately, and managed to bring the expedition to a halt by occupying the massive stronghold of Gyangtse Jong on the road to Lhasa. At this point reinforcements were summoned from India and four companies from the 1st Battalion of the Royal Fusiliers, the largest representation of British troops to be employed in the

An officer's epaulette

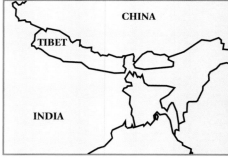

Museum displays showing the Young-husband expedition in Tibet

*Below:
The Tibet Medal
1903-04 with
clasp GYANGTSE*

expedition, helped defeat the Tibetans at Gyangtse Jong on 6th July 1904. They became the only British Regiment to fight an action at an altitude of 16,500 feet.

The Expeditionary Force entered Lhasa in August and while Colonel Younghusband conducted difficult negotiations with the Tibetans, troops fought off boredom in the primitive and squalid city with games and competitions. Finally, on September 7th, the Fusiliers escorted Younghusband into the great Potala Palace for a ceremony in which an agreement was signed with the Tibetans.

The Militia, for centuries the main defensive force of the country, was reorganised by King Charles II to make it more efficient and to bring it firmly under the control of the sovereign. The Militia gradually fell into disuse however, and on 12th May 1859 the raising of a Volunteer Force was offically authorised.

'keep up lads'

VOLUNTEERS & TERRITORIALS

1859 - 1996

Rifle Volunteer's belt buckle from the 46th Middlesex Corps

The threat of a French invasion of mainland Britain led to the formation of The Volunteer Force in 1859. The 19th Middlesex Rifle Volunteer Corps, formed in 1859 by Tom Brown of "Schooldays" fame, and the 46th Corps in 1861 became respectively in 1883 The 1st and 2nd Volunteer Battalions of Royal Fusiliers (The City of London Regiment) and adopted the dress and traditions of the parent regiment.

In 1890 they were followed by two more Battalions. All four Volunteer Battalions sent men to the South African War of 1899-1902 with The City Imperial Volunteers, The Imperial Yeomanry and Volunteer Service Companies of The Royal Fusiliers. In 1908 The London Regiment was formed as part of the Territorial Force and the first four City of London battalions were badged as Royal Fusiliers.

Officers' Undress Uniforms

From the Cyclist Section 1st Volunteer Battalion Royal Fusiliers to Captain H.C. Foulkes, in commemoration of the successes achieved by the Section under his command in 1895 & 1896 and as a token of their respect

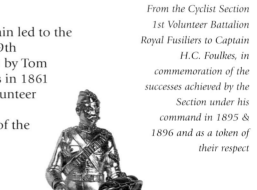

These four battalions were increased to 19 battalions during The Great War, and fought in France, Flanders, Gallipoli and Egypt, suffering severe losses in these theatres. The London Regiment underwent many changes which resulted in it being broken up in 1937.

The 3rd and 4th Battalions were converted to an artillery role, although they retained their Royal Fusilier links, while the 1st and 2nd Battalions went on to form the 8th and 9th Battalions of The Royal Fusiliers, serving with distinction during the 1939-45 War. The traditions and customs of the former Royal Fusilier Volunteers are carried on today by 'C' (City of London Fusiliers) Company, The London Regiment who are based at the former 2nd London Regiment Headquarters at Balham.

Queen Victoria's Volunteer Medal

1865

1846

1903

33

FIRST

MONS -
THE FIRST BATTLE

Britain and Germany had been at war only four days when the 4th Battalion reported itself mobilised and ready for action. Another four days later, on 12th August, the Battalion disembarked at Le Havre. Welcomed by French troops the Fusiliers responded by trying to whistle the 'Marseillaise', but soon broke into the popular Music Hall song 'Hold your hand out you naughty boy'. This, sung with great fervour and seriousness, was met by bare heads by the French, thinking after the 'Marseillaise', that it must be the British National Anthem. Unfortunately, not the last misunderstanding between allies no less staunch for being so often foes in the past.

On the 28th June 1914 a man stepped from the crowds lining the streets of Sarajevo and fired a revolver at the carriage of the Archduke Ferdinand of Austria and his wife, killing them both. Those shots plunged the whole of Europe into the First World War.

'keep up lads'

WORLD WAR 1914-1919

THE WORLD AT WAR

A month later Austria/Hungary went to war with Serbia and so activated a whole series of European Alliances.

On 4th August 1914 Great Britain declared war on Germany - a war that was to involve the whole nation and not just the regular army. It was widely believed that the war would 'be over by Christmas', but it dragged on for four long weary years, characterised by incompetence in high places, both civil and military, but relieved by the courage and heroism of the common soldier.

A German spiked helmet of the period

WORLD WAR I - THE RUN UP TO HOSTILITIES:

1. Formation of two opposing power blocks in Europe; the Triple Entente - Great Britain, France and Russia. The Triple Alliance - Germany, Austria and Italy.

2. The arms race between the two blocks.

3. The Balkans trouble spot; Austria (backed by Germany) felt threatened by Serbia (backed by Russia).

4. The Assassination of Archduke Ferdinand of Austria by a Bosnian terrorist gave Austria the pretext to attack Serbia for supporting the outrage.

5. Austria declared war on Serbia, Russia declared war on Austria, Germany declared war on Russia and France, Great Britain declared war on Germany (violation of Belgian Neutrality Treaty of 1839).

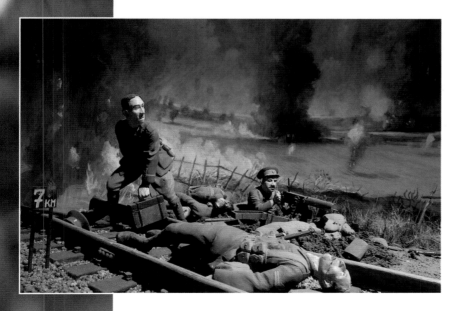

The Museum's reconstruction of Lieutenant M.J. Dease & Private S.F. Godley winning the first Victoria Crosses of World War I

By the 22nd August, the 4th Battalion was in a position on the canal bank at Mons in Belgium with Y and Z Companies facing six Battalions of the German Army. On 23rd August 1914 the 4th Battalion Royal Fusiliers was hotly engaged with advancing German troops. Lt. M.J. Dease was machine gun officer holding a position on the railway bridge on the edge of the town. The gun crews had little protection and casualties were heavy. Lt. Dease, in great pain from a bullet wound in his knee, continued to direct the fire of his guns. This meant crawling across open ground to each emplacement; he was hit at least three times and died of his wounds. He was awarded a posthumous VC. By this time all the gun crews were dead or badly wounded. Answering the call for anyone who knew how to handle a machine gun, Private S.F. Godley came forward, cleared an emplacement and brought a gun into action. Shortly afterwards the gun was hit and Private Godley badly wounded. He fell into German hands after throwing his machine gun into the canal. He was cheered in his captivity to learn that he also had been awarded the VC.

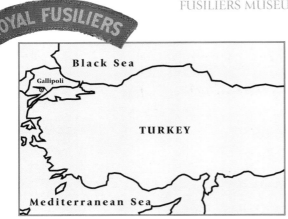

GALLIPOLI 1915 - *a costly blunder*

Turkey entered the War on the German side in late 1914, thus closing the Russian supply routes to and from the Black Sea via the Dardanelles, and launched an attack against Russia in the Caucasus mountains at the end of the year. In an effort to free the supply routes a British plan was conceived to launch a flanking movement which would push through the Dardanelles and link up with Russia, thus separating Germany from her Turkish allies. This idea was most strongly pressed by Winston Churchill as First Lord of the Admiralty, but developed into a complete disaster. By the time the 2nd Battalion of the Fusiliers, who had been in India at the beginning of the war, together with four Territorial Fusilier battalions, landed at the end of April 1915 with the first troops ashore on the narrow beaches, the Turks had had several months' warning of the Allies' intentions and were well

A dramatic interpretation of HMS Implacable in the Dardanelles, during the Gallipoli landings

prepared. The landing was a nightmare. Lieutenant Colonel Newman, commanding the Battalion, described the scene in a letter from Gallipoli:

'Very soon the ships had to stop firing on the beaches. At once the enemy opened fire, and then began such an awful carnage as I hope I may never see the like again.'

With a supreme effort, and after several episodes of extraordinary heroism, the Fusiliers secured their beach and a small area of land, but no further advance could be made. Both sides settled down to a barren trench warfare in which bloody attack alternated with bloody counter-attack. In August, the Allies tried to gain an advantage by landing troops at Suvla, behind the Turks' right flank, but initial successes were not sustained. It looked as if the efforts of the Fusiliers, whose casualties by September 14th numbered 90 officers, and 1,646 other ranks, were to count for nothing. With the coming of winter, conditions grew worse and on November 26th a flood swept over the Fusiliers' position, swirling dead Turks into the British trenches and drowning several of the Regiment. A blizzard followed the flood. Men were found the next morning dead and frozen. By the end of the month the Battalion numbered only 11 officers and 105 other ranks and orders were received to evacuate the peninsular. On January 2nd 1916 the remnants of the 2nd Battalion, Royal Fusiliers left 'W' beach. They had arrived crammed in a troopship; they left in a trawler with room to spare.

VICTORY - *the reckoning*

The German offensive had spent itself by April 1918, but the British Army was weak numerically and strategically. However, the tide was turned with the Battle of Amiens in August 1918. On 26th September the Allies attacked north of Verdun. The Germans, successively deserted by their Allies, endeavoured to obtain an armistice but by now the end was in sight. By early October the whole of the Hindenburg defences had fallen and the Allied breakthrough was complete. At the 11th hour of the 11th day of the 11th month the armistice came into effect. So ended 'The war to end all wars'. The price was high. Of 235,476 Fusiliers who took part in the war 21,941 were killed. Countless others were wounded or were taken prisoner. There were 838 decorations for gallantry awarded to men of the Regiment in that war and 842 Fusiliers were mentioned in dispatches for gallant service. This from a total of 70 Royal Fusilier battalions raised throughout the war.

Although the war was over in Europe, it was found necessary to send an Expeditionary Force to North Russia to assist the White Russian Forces. This force contained two battalions of Royal Fusiliers two of whose members won the last two Victoria Crosses of the Great War.

THE CASUALTIES		
Britain and Allies		Germany and Allies
5,013,627	KILLED	3,421,045
10,437,181	WOUNDED	8,419,533
15,450,808	TOTAL	11,840,578

They shall grow not old,
as we that are left grow old:
Age shall not weary them,
nor the years condemn.
At the going down of the sun
and in the morning
We will remember them.

IN MEMORIAM
In the Museum is a small bronze of the War Memorial created by distinguished sculptor Albert Toft which is situated at Holborn Bars, just inside the City of London, the traditional base of the Regiment. The inscription reads:

'TO THE GLORIOUS MEMORY OF THE 22000 ROYAL FUSILIERS WHO FELL IN THE GREAT WAR'

Left: Flanders 1916 The 20th Battalion pose for a photograph amidst a scene of devastation

CAMPAIGNS IN
THE SECOND
WORLD WAR

During the 1939-
1945 War
Battalions of the
Royal Fusiliers took
part in the following
campaigns:

FRANCE 1940

THE DEFENCE OF
BRITAIN 1940-41

THE MIDDLE
EAST AND SYRIA
1939-43

WESTERN
DESERT AND
IRAQ 1943-44

NORTH WEST
AFRICA 1942-43

ITALY 1943-45

1939-1945
Star

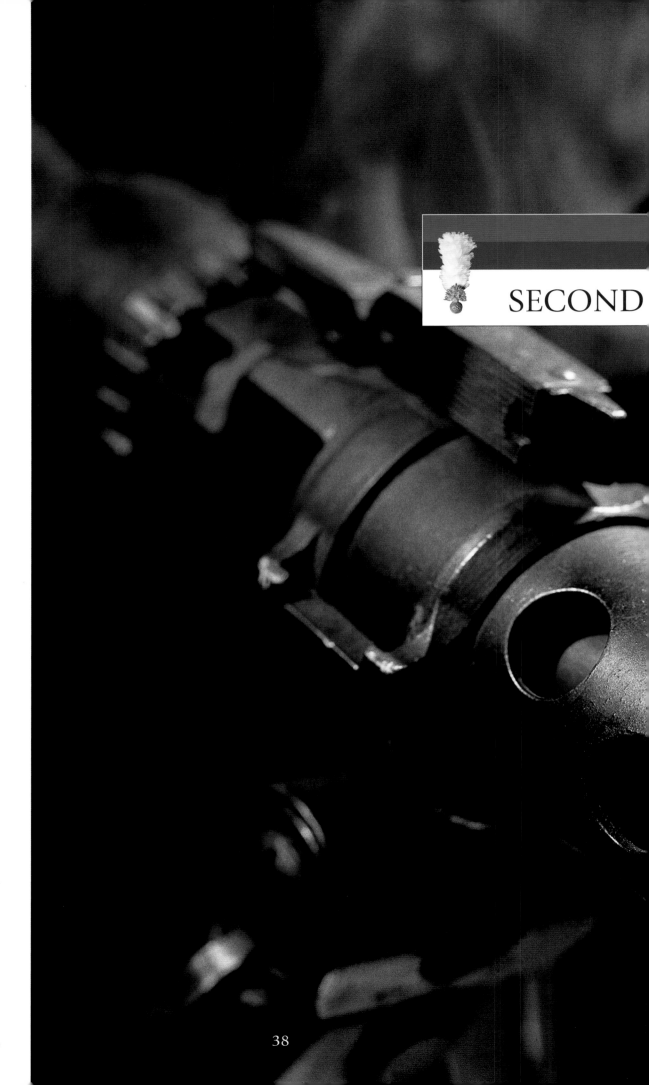

SECOND

The history of the Royal Fusiliers from 1939 shows an infantry regiment gradually adapting itself to swiftly changing types of warfare, with flexibility and adaptability replacing endurance as the prime virtues of the infantryman.

A Royal Fusilier's combat helmet with bullet hole

'keep up lads'

WORLD WAR 1939-1945

RETURN TO THE WESTERN FRONT

An early version of the standard issue combat helmet for the German soldier of WWII - showing the ventilation holes

The great infantry masses of the First World War were no longer required; in the Second World War only 17 Fusilier battalions were formed, not all of which saw active service. Many battalions were transformed and given new functions - for example the 10th Battalion became a search-light regiment, and others became anti-aircraft, anti-tank or reconnaissance units. Fusiliers regretted the changes, not unnaturally, but quickly came to see their value.

The 2nd Battalion were engaged throughout the withdrawal through Belgium and France where the remnants were evacuated from the beaches at Dunkirk.

India Ltd. 'V for Victory' cigarettes

The Africa Star

FIGHTING ROMMEL'S ARMY - *the western desert*

Joining the 'Desert Rats'

Like the 1st Battalion, the 8th and 9th Battalions were kept active and on the move through the Middle-Eastern and African campaign. Arriving in Kirkuk in December 1942 they were deployed to guard the vital Anglo-Iraqi oil installations in Syria. In early 1943, they were ordered to join the 8th Army in North Africa to deliver what it was hoped would be the final blow to Rommel's forces. In January 1943 they were joined by the 2nd Battalion, now reformed and retrained after its losses at Dunkirk. Despite the fierceness of much of the fighting, the harshness of the desert and the situations of lonely danger which the modern soldier was increasingly coming to experience as part of his everyday work, the Fusiliers kept up their morale and discipline.

The Desert Rats!

A standard issue Colt .45 Service revolver

SUCCESS AT SIDI BARRANI

At the outbreak of war the 1st Battalion had been stationed at Jhansi in India for two years and was recognised to be the best British Battalion in Eastern Command. When it was ordered to North Africa to fight the Italians the Commander-in-Chief wrote to the Battalion 'I wish I were to be with you. You'll earn more laurels to your Regimental record, which is hard to beat'. But even the C-in-C could not have foreseen the speed and decisiveness with which those laurels would be won. As soon as the Battalion had crushed the Italians at the Battle of Sidi Barrani in December 1940 their division, the 4th Indian Division, was withdrawn and sent posthaste to dispatch the Italians from Sudan, Eritrea and Abyssinia.

THE ITALIAN CAMPAIGN

'Donald Duck' was the Italian mascot and pet of the 9th Battalion Royal Fusiliers when in Italy 1944. The bird was in fact a female pochard duck

The Allied landings at Salerno and later at Anzio, with enormous quantities of weapons and equipment and strong support from the RAF, showed that the lessons of Gallipoli had been learnt, but soon the Fusiliers had to learn new skills.

Sergeant Myall recalled watching the 9th Battalion coming under fire:

'We advanced out of the olive groves completely into the open and I've never seen the Battalion so grand. They advanced in their section formations just as if it was a manoeuvre ... I've always been proud of my Battalion and knew they would uphold the fine traditions of the Regiment'

One great obstacle lay in the path of the Allies' advance on Rome - Monte Cassino. This mountain-top monastery now fortified by the Germans, totally dominated the main land route through the Liri valley. Cassino illustrated the unchanging role of the Infantry. One Fusilier wrote home:

'Then, soon after the attack went in, it rained. Supplies struggled up the mule path and wounded men slithered down under continuous shelling. That journey was no lover's lane, dead and stinking mules, wounded being carried down who were re-wounded, their bearers probably killed, lying groaning until such time as someone found them'.

That description of Cassino in 1944 could equally have described the Fusiliers at Albuhera in 1811, New Orleans in 1814 or Mons in 1914. Such scenes were to be re-enacted later in the Second World War and again in the Korean conflict.

Left: Friend and foe alike - wounded British and German soldiers are carried through Cassino to receive medical attention

Main picture: A 75mm gun on a Sherman tank fires to silence German sniper fire from the devastated buildings of Cassino as a British soldier waits to attack

*Photographs courtesy of
The Trustees of the Imperial War Museum
NA14985 & NA13805*

THE BATTLE OF MONTE CASSINO 1943-4

On December 2nd the 167th Brigade began the attack on the 300 foot high Monte Cassino, the 1st and 2nd Battalions fighting almost alongside each other, reunited for the first time since 1919.

One Fusilier recalled the climb to the mountain rendezvous: 'On the final stages men..... were so exhausted that there had to be a halt and rest approximately every ten minutes. At each halt one officer near me was prostrate on the rocks, vomiting from exhaustion ...
But all reached the top'.

It is the ultimate mark of Regimental virtuosity when a Battalion can fight imperturbably in the most trying physical circumstances and still keep to the timing of a complicated battle. This is what the Fusiliers did at Monte Cassino, and the ultimate victory owed much to their discipline, courage and skill. Lieutenant Colonel Black, who was commanding the 152nd Field Regiment R.A. wrote on May 14th to Lt. Colonel Evans of the 2nd Fusiliers:

'Forgive my presumption, but I do wish to say how magnificent I thought the attack by your Battalion was yesterday. From my O.P. on Trocchio one overlooks the whole valley and I never wish to see a more perfectly executed attack'.

The Italy Star

41

Right: Conditions in Korea often required specialised precautions - Parka, Balaclava helmet, goggles

United Nations Medal for Korea

The Queen's Medal for Korea

KOREA

42

In June 1950 Communist North Korea invaded South Korea. The United Nations responded by sending troops, including a British contingent.

'keep up lads'

1950-1951

Sometimes tension and distrust erupt into war. Then the soldier has a puzzling task. The war must be kept limited; no one must be given even half a reason for dropping an atomic bomb.

Two exhausted Fusiliers rest in a ditch in Korea

The idea is not to 'win' the war, but to continue fighting until a settlement can be agreed which will stop the war. Yet, on the other hand, these limited affairs are used to test the readiness and flexibility of coventional forces in the event of an atomic war. Korea pointed out the nature of the dilemma. The Royal Fusiliers landed in Korea in August 1952 and left in August 1953. By the time they arrived the pattern of the war had been well established. In a sense it had become an unreal war, depending on a set of tacit agreements between the two sides as to what was possible and what was not, almost as formal as an 18th century engagement.

For the good of humanity this was as well, and President Truman no doubt did right to sack General MacArthur when his military ambition outran his commonsense. But to expect a Regiment to learn anything new and relevant to the atomic age under these circumstances was unrealistic.

Among the many privations suffered by the Battalion, 'Operation Pimlico', the one operation of any size in which the Regiment took part, was unnecessary, although the Fusiliers fought with their customary bravery. Fusilier Hodgkinson was awarded an immediate Distinguished Conduct Medal for his bravery in this battle.

A light machine gun of Chinese manufacture captured during the conflict

NORTHERN IRELAND

On 23rd April 1968, the Royal Northumberland Fusiliers, the Royal Warwickshire Fusiliers, the Royal Fusiliers and the Lancashire Fusiliers were merged into a new large regiment, The Royal Regiment of Fusiliers with four regular battalions. Economies to the Army have steadily reduced the number to two regular battalions today.

RIFLE 5·56mm XL85E2

NORTHERN
IRELAND

REPUBLIC
OF IRELAND

*NORTHERN
IRELAND*

Although tours of duty in Northern Ireland might be seen as routine to an onlooker they are not so to a serving Fusilier who continues to maintain the traditions of his regiment whilst helping to maintain the Queen's Peace in that unhappy country. His patience, skill and forbearance are placed at the service of all the inhabitants no matter on which side of the sectarian divide they belong.

The first Battalion of Fusiliers to serve in Northern Ireland since the present troubles began arrived in June 1970

Two Fusiliers enjoy themselves amongst the community in Northern Ireland

The Fusiliers have completed over 30 operational tours in Northern Ireland since 1970. Fourteen Fusiliers have been killed on duty in the Province and many more wounded. However, their comrades have continued to carry out their duties with the Fusiliers usual cheerfulness and dedication to duty.

On 14th September, Britain declared its intention to send a large force to join the allied forces in Saudi Arabia and on 12th December the 3rd Battalion, the Royal Regiment of Fusiliers, began moving from Germany to the Gulf to reinforce the British contingent.

'keep up lads'

THE GULF   1990-91

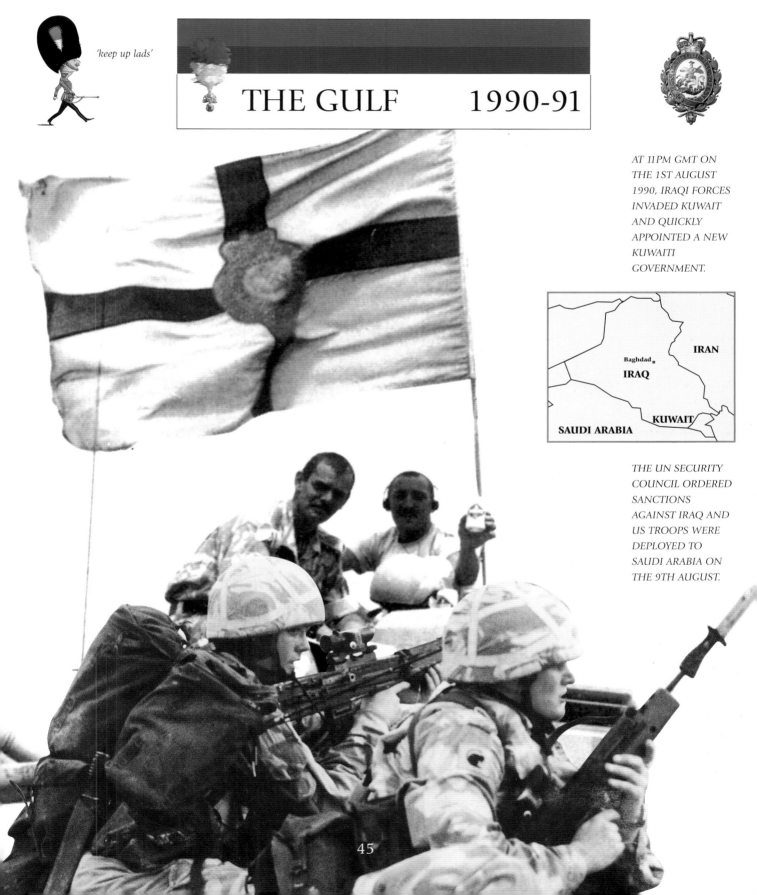

AT 11PM GMT ON THE 1ST AUGUST 1990, IRAQI FORCES INVADED KUWAIT AND QUICKLY APPOINTED A NEW KUWAITI GOVERNMENT.

IRAN

Baghdad

IRAQ

KUWAIT

SAUDI ARABIA

THE UN SECURITY COUNCIL ORDERED SANCTIONS AGAINST IRAQ AND US TROOPS WERE DEPLOYED TO SAUDI ARABIA ON THE 9TH AUGUST.

The 3rd Battalion Battle Group, under the command of Lt. Col. A.L.D. de H. Larpent, then commenced further intensive training prior to advancing into Iraq on 25th February at the start of the ground war.

OPERATION DESERT STORM

Fusiliers of 2 Platoon, A company, take a breather with their Warrior

The 3rd Battalion on the march in the Gulf

Lieutenant Sharon O'Connor, the only woman serving with the 3rd Battalion in the Gulf

INTO BATTLE

Although the ground war was short and sharp, the 3rd Fusiliers were in constant touch with the Iraqi forces throughout and played a full part in the advance.

General Schwarzkopf addressing the 3rd Battalion RRF on 30th March 1991

Sadly, during the final phases, the Battalion sustained serious casualties including nine killed, when two of their Warrior armoured vehicles were destroyed by 'friendly fire' from allied airplanes.

The Fusiliers' efforts were recognised by the award of two Battle Honours 'Gulf 1991' and 'Wadi al Batin' and the following individual awards: 1 DSO, 1 CBE, 1 MBE, 1 MC, 1 QGM, 1 BEM, 1 MID.

HM The Queen approved the award of THE MILITARY CROSS to Captain Anthony Guy Briselden 3rd Battalion

A row of Campaign medals from The Gulf, Northern Ireland and Bosnia

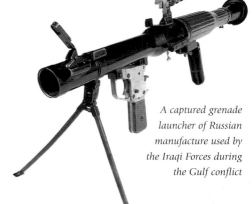

A captured grenade launcher of Russian manufacture used by the Iraqi Forces during the Gulf conflict

Right: An IFOR armoured vehicle escorts a horse and cart along a bleak mountain road in Bosnia

'keep up lads'

THE BALKANS

BOSNIA

As a result of the break up of Yugoslavia, an inter-ethnic war raged in Bosnia between April 1992 and October 1995. At that time a UN Force was put in place to pave the way for stability and progress. Both regular Battalions of the Fusiliers have served in Bosnia, the 1st Battalion from August 1995 to March 1996, and the 2nd Battalion from May to November 1997 with the UN and the subsequent NATO Force. During these tours The Fusiliers rose to the challenge magnificently earning a justifiably fine reputation throughout the region, the Army and the Government.

Left: Three Fusiliers consult a map in Bosnia; their red and white hackles distinctive against the background

THE ROYAL REGIMENT OF FUSILIERS MUSEUM

Fusiliers outside the Museum with the Regimental Mascot

The Museum is open from 9.30am to 5.30pm Monday to Saturday 10.30am to 5.30pm Sunday during the Summer.

9.30am to 4.30pm Monday to Saturday 10.30am to 4.30pm Sunday during the Winter.

The Museum is closed on Christmas Day and New Year's Day.

There is a Museum Shop which has a wide range of Regimental souvenirs, prints and fine china that appeals to the young and not so young alike.

The Officers' Mess at Regimental Headquarters dressed 'for dinner'

A Fusilier dressed 'for action'

Due to the present nature of the building and the exhibition we regret that there are no facilities for the disabled.

'nice one lads!'